cop.1

294.3443 Reps, Paul, 1895-
R   Juicing : Words and brushwork / by
         Paul Reps. — Garden City, N.Y. :
         Anchor Books, 1978.
            111 p. : ill. ; 21 cm.

            ISBN 0-385-13250-6

            1. Zen meditations.   I. Title.
BQ9289.5.R46   294.3'4'43
                                         77-82770
                                         MARC

Library of Congress
01295   PE   659523   © THE BAKER & TAYLOR CO.   8353

skin.
of onion
thinking

JUICING

words and brushwork

by paul reps

Anchor Books
Doubleday & Company, Inc.
Garden City, New York, U.S.A.
1978

Anchor Books edition: 1978

Library of Congress Cataloging in Publication Data

Reps, Paul, 1895—
    Juicing.

    1. Zen meditations.   I. Title.
BQ9289.5.R46   294.3'4'43
ISBN: 0-385-13250-6
Library of Congress Catalog Card Number 77—82770

CONTENTS

Making sense through our electroflow cosmos

—Amerindian weaving

PRE-FACE

This book gives
somethings to let do
already doing
to have you as new
all through

It completes
on each page
Open anywhere
Also open you

"Why do a book cultivating me
when nuclear war — lack of fresh air —
starvation — disease — unease — fake food
are falling on us fast?"

Agreed
We face a life/death reality
How to face it subjects this work
                    .

It proposes a new orienting —
not kill but let —
not apart but including
other life forms with ours —
not out-think but feel

We need a new human on earth
Could this new human be you?

1 JUICING

Without juices
we would be
recluses

Let eyes close
let lips touch
Taste
Feel juices
transforming

We are 80% fluidic
        90% light
       100% us

Would you like to feel good all through?
Sweeten your juices   nerveflowjuice
                       bloodflowjuice
                       lymphflowjuice
                       vitalflowjuice

You have the power to sweeten or sour
your juiceflow at once   and do

Your cells respond as you

Lavish statement:
                Our body has one trillion
                (1,000 billion) cells
                each one wiser than we are
                each immersed in all-conscious
                protoplasm

Another way to be good to your juiceflow:

Stop complaining

Start thanking

use
your
FLOWER mind

2 SOFTENING

"Where do I hear music?"

In me

"Where do I feel pain?"

In me

This book reports instances

of learning for me

You cannot touch or taste for me

But I can

You cannot see or hear for me

But I can

During my lifetime so far

I have known magnificent exemplars

but they were helpless to learn for me

This book shows me learning

Indulgence weakens

INTEGRITY strengthens seeing

I see a mountain
      INsee myself climbing it

If I INsee myself not climbing
I'm not going to make it

We name this faith and doubt
moving our mouth like a professor

May we actually INsee and INhear
distant events?

Indians of the upper Amazon can
Yogins of India have done so for centuries
A mother somehow INsees her distant child

One sense interweaves with another
although our sensings are mostly out of use

                    May we graduate through sensing?
                    After total release of seeing
                    looking from where SEEING looks
                    what do we see?

                    "SEEING"

                    Right   Yet as I say "I see it"
                    and overlook SEEING
                    I tangle in "I" and "it"
                    and am hooked as a fish
                    out of water

                    Fish IN water is the SEEING

SEE SOME OBJECT AT EYE LEVEL
CLOSE EYES AND SEE SOME OBJECT
IN YOUR IMAGINATION

How do these experiences differ?
No imaging without imagining
no imagining without imaging
both are inexplicably subtle
more inspiriting than mattering

We live in our imaging-imagining
unconsciously and may do so
consciously

Once we realize this our whole
life changes for the better
as we change it

QUIET DOWN IN A QUIET PLACE
AND IMAGE-IMAGINE SOMETHING
EXTREMELY GOOD FOR YOU
AS ALREADY COMING ABOUT

What we image we imagine
and what we imagine we image

As we use low power energy to
telephone someone on other side
of world so our imaging-imagining
turns on our very good

May we say it evidences us as spirit
or as something finer than dense
matter?

LET BREATHFLOW FLOW
NATURALLY OUT–IN   OUT–IN
AND H U M M WITH OUTBREATHFLOW
AND R E C E I V E
(YOUR BEST POSSIBILITY)
WITH INBREATHFLOW

This amazing low power practice
electrics us

3 PAUSING

The longer the pause
the fewer the flaws

In the pause your nerve
network resting in
consummate ease

Imagine pause as a vitamin
as big as an elephant

"Why pause?"
Why go out of breath?

Breath paused
heart paused
heart paused
life paused
into the next moment life

We pause between words said
in slow step
seeing   hearing   replying
as bliss this

Need you run about
unguided?

If you don't guide you
who will?

If you guide you can you
compute the uncounted
strings tying your
exquisite package
together?
        — rosebud conversation

who
is

To brighten eyesight
fill mouth with water
and splash water over eyes
Empty mouth
Lower head slowly

Wait
witness beauty of leaf
pause
harmony of sound
tip of nose   fragrance
tip of tongue   flavor
middle of tongue   touch
root of tongue   sound
flex toes
touch fingertips
joints juicing
who shall you thank
for such gifts
the wholly one ?

surprise

is your
head
on
straight?

Inner exploring:
What am I about between thoughts?
Energizing or de-energizing?
Stopping the war?
Jettisoning baggage?
Loving Mr and Ms God?
Planting a tree?
Deep smiling?

You are burned
Your skin rejects my skin graft
yet welcomes yours

Find guidance within
companion without
near
dear

This work asks attention of your be-ing
not your superior thinking
Your thoughts do   know you are you
Your feelings do   . know you are you

When you stop to locate you
you find experiencing infiniting spacious changing free
including "you" and "me"

                                        Feel head float up
                                        from back

                                        (releases jaw)
                                        (depressures)

Standing
free
feel weight
more on one foot
then on the other
s l o w l y
then
on both feet

up legs

up back

wholeheartedly

Keep here

Let head rest loosely
on chest

Let it swing a little
to right   to left
as the pendulum of a clock

As your other motions
are so loose and swingy
you are ready to live
(this book)

Until
it's fun
it's better
left undone

4 STANDING

Head floating up from back
eyesoft   jawloose
soft-kneed   inlightly

heels touching
as if about to go
three ways at once
let   weight forward
into balls of feet
and without stepping
swing both heels out
so feet are parallel
for integrity and apart
for stability

strong

tireless

primitive

Arms reaching high
close to ears
loosening neck
s l o w l y
lower arms
to sides

Keep
high

an inch off middle

standing
in the
bottom
of our
feet

5 SIT

It's raining dewing sprinkling
showers of golden light so fine
so pure so INvigorating
      wherever you sit

S

T

I

L

L

First we are in a jungle
and very alert

then there are books
and we get heady

now there's tell-vision
and we see more and
insight less

Do we need a new   INsee
                    INlight
                    INjoy

a new human on earth?

Difficult?
Lie down
Release tight areas
Sit and do likewise

Chair never declares "I am a chair"
Object has no awareness   Subject *is*

6   MOVING

smooth

as if to some silent music

s l o w l y   evenly

IN   unbreaking motion

Feel

a motion

about to move you

Can you move smooth?

You can and do

using fine and finer nerve-muscles

Can you open a door silently?
Can you walk without hurry worry?
Can you turn around and then move surely yet softly?
Can you move descending gravity (love)
and ascending lightness above waist?

Examples of low-powered moving :
An idea
A way you open this book
Bud opening

In comparison   forcing   ache   pain
seem high-powered installations

Remember that each motion
we make frees or binds us

"How?"

Even as we move over in
sleep we free us

In waking our motion binds us
only as we hold on to it

WHAT WE DO MOST
MOVE
WE GIVE LEAST ATTENTION

You do move   don't you?
If you move find a way
that comes to you directly
to move you   out of
your troubling

"But how?"
Move at an even s l o w
tempo as tree turns in
wind   as flower moves
toward sun

In the position you're in
begin to turn s l o w l y
and keep on turning
s l o w l y   farther than
possible

This produces a stretch
Just after you reverse   it
and begin to turn the
other way   you are free
of me   of the one who
says "me"

There are hundreds of motions
in your one-day adventure
you may do this with

Walk inside a room
inside your skin
inside nerve-muscles
moving only the nerve
sheath   s l o w l y

Like walking on air

Some airports have soft
floors with round
platelike protrusions
so everyone walks
silently   in a new
dimension

As you move continue
experimenting with smooth
self motion spontaneously
generating
non-repetitive
fresh

Do not accept ANY stale
second-hand motion imposed
on you by another or by
you

WHY ARE SO MANY HUMANS
UNHAPPY WHEN THEY CAN
MOVE SMOOTH?
Why do others ritualize
possess and impose motions
on us when we can injoy
living motion freshly?

If the world ship sinks
will you save it?
Yes you will
Move smooth

We each has some special bind
neck stiff   /   shoulders rigid/
jaw set   /   knees stiff/
feet bound   /   face ominous/

Then we move against it
fighting ourself   looking old
souring juices   our bloodflow
blocks   creases appear
signaling imprisonments

Learning we may unknot the
world in us our bones sinews
ligaments   respond

What could be easier than to
m o v e ?   Experiment
discover some best way to make
a given motion with least
effort   no matter how long it
takes

Simply to feel
a congestion
and keep feeling
begins to release it

Our pills and potions
and non-herb foods
back up on us when we
forget to move

Considerately moving
you are your own best
friend

Unknot   world in you

SMOOTH MOTION
CURES COMMOTION

smooth: even   steady   unbreaking
motion   :   a melting of one position into another
cures   :   relieves
commotion: fear   suffering

Whenever you feel uncomfortable what do you do?
You move   Whenever you feel joyfull you move

Consider this   opportunity
Entering moving   our separate self melts

Intent moves us
Moving without intent would be
as marriage without love
mere exercise

Does your moving flow with others?
Does the "you" in it melt with all-life?

Be faster than think
think faster than feel
feel faster than do
why then move slow?

Not fast   not slow
      invisibly evenly
as old garments falling
away   nakedly innocently
Is this how new humans are born?

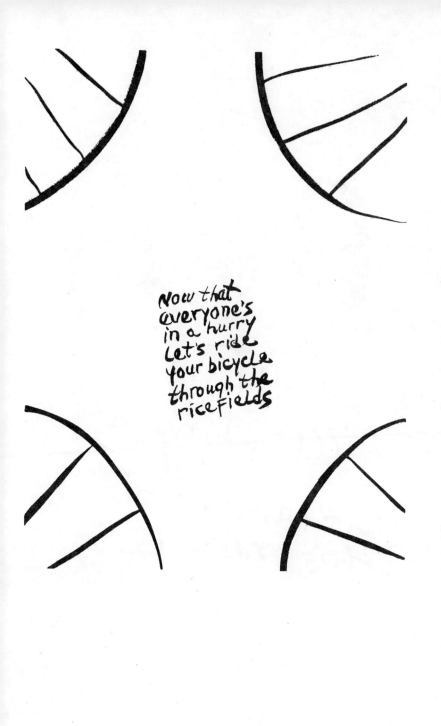

Now that
everyone's
in a hurry
Let's ride
your bicycle
through the
rice fields

A A

Lift

Little fingers *

who can ex-plain
this miracle?

7 LET

The more
you are you
the fuller
breathflow flows

When someone
in-vites you to tea
keep moving
deliciously

Breathflow
circling
down front
up back
    (scrubs back)

Let
breathflow flow
as you do
in your rhythm of suns and seas
given with your conception

    As water
    f   l   o   w   s

       IN

    the great harmony

All we need do

– to be breathed –

with outbreathflow equal to

inbreathflow

Few accomplish this even once in a lifetime

You can go a long time without drinking or eating

but only a few minutes without breathing
Breathflow must be   most primary action
in rhythm with your radiance interpenetrating
matter   Even a stone radiates   breathes

Your breathflow reflects you immediately
If you run fast it comes fast   and when you
slow down   breathflow slows down

It will vary from morning to noon and from noon
to midnight   If you tighten up it will
tighten to flow around   self-imposed knots

Breathflow pauses when you pause
this pause built in your nature

Welcome but do not try to pause it
by imposing something yet imperfect on
something perfect
Just let breathflow flow

As you do your bloodstream oxygenates more
thoroughly   rests more exquisitely
With oxygen assimilation   enhanced
you may be well   weller
in a few days
How wonderful

Discovery

Feel
breathflow evenly
out-in   out-in
and actually feel
this gift of life
with each
inbreathflowing

Not refined motion
nor re-found motion
but motion dedicated
to our cosmos good
will be understood

How many breathflow
have you in your
24 hours?
"About 14,400"
What are you planting
into them?

8 STRETCHING

A slight smile
stretches a mile

Turn s l o w l y evenly to right
a little farther than possible
s t r e t c h i n g

then s l o w l y the other way
evenly   farther than possible
       Discover
       INlight
       just after a sustained stretch
S l o w l y arms stretch
neck   back   legs
in-vent   in-joy stretches
Any motion may be stretched
Or   hang from limb of tree
s l o w l y

s   t   r   e   t   c   h

In back   with eyes closed
totally at ease
hands resting on abdomen under ribcage
feel   deep indrawing of vital energy
with inbreathflow through nostrils
then with outbreathflow
squeeze navel to backbone
radiating   stored   energy
through every lightpoint cell hair tissue
for 100 miles around in all directions
44 times

Very welling
May be the rightest of motions
(What were you visualizing for you
before you read this?)

slowly raise and lower
each segment of backbone
until only shoulders and feet
on ground

Flexive = young
stiff = old
choose

Youth the world over
make some slight low-powered adjustment
to feel good

Change skin
brushing it under water

Whatever troubles
let it through
without reacting to it

Whatever pleases
let it through
without reacting to it

nothing is the matter

ant to ant:

"ant!"

9 SQUEEZE

SQUEEZE hands tight
open bright
grassblade light

Only hands?
As we squeeze
we squeeze all through

The law
Exert with outbreathflow
receive with inbreathflow

releasing face
while opening hands

releasing shoulders
while opening hands

releasing body base
while opening hands

Constrictions dissolve
congestions vanish
Nothing could be
more important

Kneeling
touch head to ground
(9 times)
Lowest becomes highest
(squeezes guts)
(feels good)
    don't do it for any
reason   If you do
something for some reason
you are put out
Be found IN whatever
"it" is

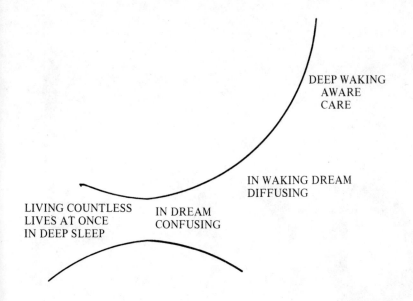

DEEP WAKING
AWARE
CARE

IN WAKING DREAM
DIFFUSING

LIVING COUNTLESS
LIVES AT ONCE   IN DREAM
IN DEEP SLEEP   CONFUSING

"good" "good" "good"
outdoors walking morning
evening
out of the get
into the walk

Right hand over left
rest assured
(then over other
frightened areas)

Do you know there are
100,000,000 galaxies
within the range of our
100-inch telescope?

One leaf
in ground
can grow a
tree

As new all through
in 5 seconds
Sit
in tub of cold water
(shocks blood circulation)
(cools hot head)

Sleep deep
Will not to will

Wake
Will

Suppose you will it a tree
Tree is not tree to tree
Look
See the tree

You see it
but someone kicks you
You kick back
WILL withdraws tree
for kick

Thus you go around
making worlds while
WILL makes you

We choose (will) the tempo and rhythm we gesture (move)
It happens so fast we miss this choice so descend into
desire for something already given

As we choose a slower rhythm we become tone and music
re-turning to our cosmos rhythm   wherein all are moving
dancing   still

Moving gently with heartflow
opens breathflow

encourages rhythmic circulation
loosens nerves of backbones
decelerates
depressures
unknots the worlds in us

      SIT
      STILL

      LET EYE-JERKS QUIET

      LET BREATHFLOW FLOW

Somehow wherever we are tight
starts to loosen
and lower back begins to
straighten   as a child's
healthier
stronger

Professional (zen) sitters
over world find this to be so

Why not?
Anyone can still
Anyone can cease eye-jerking
Anyone can feel breathflow rhythm
Anyone can transcend talk-back

10 EAT

To breath LIGHT
open nostrils

To end starvation on earth
eat air
close eyes when chewing
share

      Can you fast from food?
      You do so each night
      Can you fast from possessing?
      You learn to
      Can you fast from breathflow?
      In breathflow pause
      Can you fast from death?
      Born   as we are   each moment

         Drinking water
         water drinks me

         breathing air
         air breathes me

         experiencing LIGHT
         INlights me

To eat air
draw air in through tongue
curled as a tube
swallow

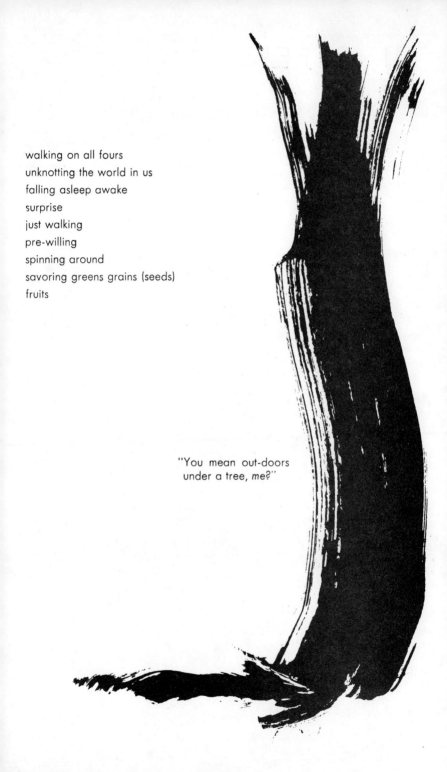

walking on all fours
unknotting the world in us
falling asleep awake
surprise
just walking
pre-willing
spinning around
savoring greens grains (seeds)
fruits

"You mean out-doors
under a tree, *me?*"

11　SLEEP

being   BEING
BEING   being

In deep sleep
hybernation

  one life
sapping

bud
adoring
sun

12 WAKING

How can life be as sweet
as   when all our
troublings dissolve?

You know how
You fall asleep each night
Why not fall awake?

Fact:

No one sees
We are shown "it"   "it"
in INlight so fast
it seems motionless
true as you

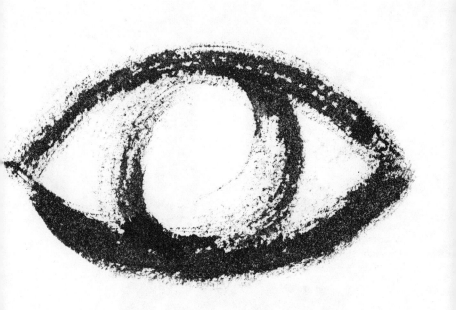

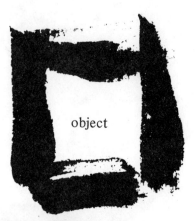

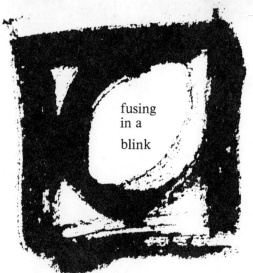

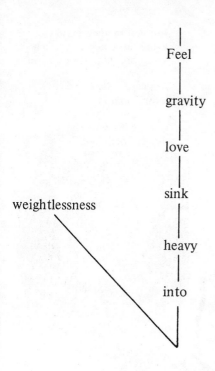

Feel

gravity

love

sink

heavy

into

weightlessness

Softly shake
    arms
    hands
    legs
    feet
    shoulders
    wake

HOW TO HELP LET THIS BOOK
HELP MAKE A NEW
HUMAN ON EARTH

Consider it deeply
alonely   slightly hungry

Throw it away if it
fails to feed you the
kind of food you hunger for

Find it   years later
Look again
Open to the page for you
Change the practice to
accord with you according
Ask   ask consideringly
how   how   how
      let let let

IN   a changing cosmos
WITH everything changing
you are sure to change too

Swirl   whirl how
extraordinarily ordinary

unchange

55

Are you reading these words?
What are you doing to them?
What are they doing to you?

Are they tightening or
loosening you

as a gentle breeze
across your cheek?

Bird flies
fish swims
he she's
she hims

surprise

are you
in here
somewhere?

Standing
loosen arms
neck
   breathflow
inbreathflow arms rising
softly to sides
as wings
opening
to fly

Look at you
cells lighter

Each one is best
best
best
unique in uniquity each offers
something rare
no two pebbles leaves snowflakes
times places faces
the same
            fresh too

no
two
Snowflakes

If you like starting
and joining
why not start and join

"I won't kill"
International

No dues   no obligations

When enough of us so declare
and mean it mutation will annul
munition and weapon manufacture
for good

Start with you
Those near pick it up
and as earth turns
those on the other side

These words already are spoken
in the hearts of common folk
the world over who have had
their fill of politicians
and exploiters and are about
to give them notice
"I won't kill"

deep sleep deep waking

In football
they huddle together
whisper a number
then
         SHIFT

Ball passed
play starts
everyone runs somewhere

Reading/thinking this
can you shift from
think to
         FEEL

         as a team of one?

GAME OF REVELATIONS

Flying before leaving ground
speaking before making sound
two humans share their
revelations
whatever comes

The truer revelation wins

Youth already plays this game
world over   shaping a future
presently

LET THERE BE
TRANSLUCENT DWELLINGS
ONE POSTAL SYSTEM
ONE AIR NETWORK
ONE TALK SPREAD
ONE CURRENCY
ONE WORLD ORDER
MULTIPLE SMALL BOXES
OF SUN POWER FUSING
FREE ENERGY
NO ONE STARVING
NO ONE KILLING
YET UNHAPPY LACKING
INNER DIRECTIVE
THEN YOU DEEP WAKING
APPEAR

The day goes by when we can live separatively as primitives
as   arrogant english   prolific africans
familial chinese   consummate japanese   otherworld hindus
joyful mexicans   do-it-better north americans
wholehearted hawaiians   ecstatic tahitians   romantic arabs
frugal norwegians   regimented swedes
as many expressions on one face
There are many kinds of trees

From
everywhere
Living
on earth

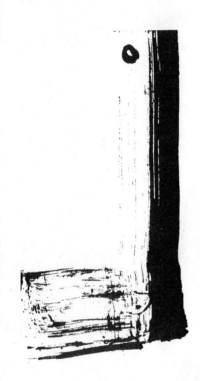

open,
doors

walking
through forest
I rearrange
the trees

13 STEMMING

on your back
place hands under head
as a pillow

observation:
when doing this
did you lift head too?

tightening brainstem
from tophead to body base?

Does human discomfort and war
start here?
Does violence begin with
self violence?

See how young child or cat
leaves brainstem loose
while moving

slide hands under *inert* head
as a pillow
good stemming

I have no parents
I make heaven and earth my parents

I have no home
I make awareness my home

I have no life or death
I make breath tides my life and death

I have no divine power
I make integrity my divine power

I have no means
I make understanding my means

I have no magic secret
I make honesty my magic secret

I have no body
I make endurance my body

I have no eyes
I make the lighting flash my eyes

I have no ears
I make sensibility my ears

I have no limbs
I make promptness my limbs

I have no strategy
I make unshadowed-by-thought my strategy

I have no designs
I make opportunity my design

I have no miracles
I make right action my miracles

I have no principles
I make adaptability my principles

I have no tactics
I make emptiness/fullness my tactics

I have no friends
I make you   mind   friends

I have no enemy   I have no castle
I make carelessness my enemy   I make heaven/earth my castle

I have no armor   I have no sword
I make compassion my honor   I make absence of self my sword

—14th-century Samurai

On back   knees up
let legs swing together slowly
far to right   then to left
(loosening brainstem at bottom)

Let head turn slowly to right
then far left
(loosening at top)

                    tree
                    receiving untold news
                    through these roots
                    delight through leaves
                    windblown flexively
                    beyond suffering
                    beyond bliss
                    this

With deep respect for   Toward the one
(great nature)   the perfecting of
Japanese farmers bow   love harmony beauty
before small wood shrines   the only being —
in the ricefields   — invocation of
(silently thanking)   sufi inayat khan

Since men STILL make war
Let me lie down and sing
with the grasses

OVERFLOW

To overflow
do nothing at all

If you do something
you only use up energy
self-filling as you
let it
(as in deep sleep)

As energy overflows
    feel good

How simple   how profound
Let it
Do nothing
while doing something

A room without a shrine
or centering also drains
energy
Have one picture or none
in it   Honor the image
Make room

Where are you going
with your finest instrument?
Here?   There?
Do you know who guides you
to each here?
Have you already arrived?
Who sits in your seat?

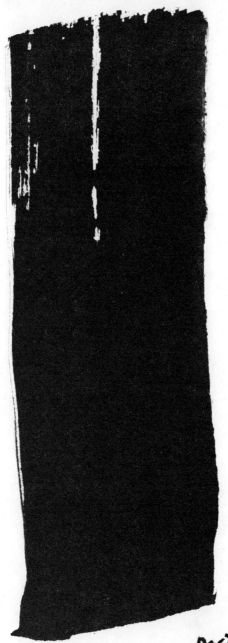

post
buddha

14 INSINGING

To hide the tribe's position
Amerindian mother holds
the child's mouth shut
Mother   hold mine

We communicate with words
commune with

S I L E   N   C   I   N   G

They say old yoga and Buddha taught
to meditate while sitting and walking
placing attention IN   what one thinks
or does   then naming it

"sitting   sitting"

"breathing   breathing"

"moving   moving"

as skin of onion thinking

In China and in Japan sitters sat
without even naming it
In Tibet   smelled intoned sensed it

To two most ancient yogas of light
and sound we would   add a third   MOTION
that becomes LIGHTING   SOUNDING   MOVING
as we let it

An African moves superbly
How do you move?

A Chinese shakes hands
from heart   means it
How do you shake hands?

INlight   :   lightness

Silent sound   :   Cup hands over nose
inhear breathflow

Cup hands over ears
inhear cell purring

this innate sound in wind   sea
hum of insects   of motor   auuummm
through every word of every language
ever-ly

they are
all singing
only we
don't hear
them

                    We yawn   ah
                    exclaim oh
        we   eeeee
            coo   uuuu

SILENT SOUND
NOH SOUND
WE ARE

Sub-silent sound
eeeeeeeeeeeeee   electric
aaaaaahhhhhhhh   energizing
ooooooooooohhhh   enfolding
uuuuuuuuuuuuuu   revealing

B	body	
C	expressive	Consonant shaping
D	determined	
F	flourishing	
G	getting	
H	organizing	
I	ah-ee	
J	leading	
K	unexpecting	
L	traveling	
M	molding	
N	nervelighting	
P	apperceiving	
Q	qualifying	
R	understanding	
S	intensifying	
T	refining	
V	versatile	
W	wavering	
X	self sign	
Y	quieting	
Z	compressing	

shrieking
torn from stem
the flower

gives its life for me
What else may I do
but give my life to you

15 INLIGHTING

We touch a button
to light a room
What button may we touch
to INlight us?

Rebirth in LIGHT

Place 100 fine gold screens
one on top of another

From above blow LIGHT through

One lightdrop appears
it's YOU

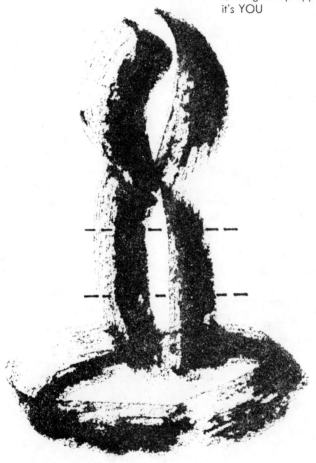

Facing you (or object)
and you me
both looking softly through
without eye-jerking
INlight

> Who is that effulgent one
> directing eye to form and
> ear to sound?
> —Upanishad

May we turn from seeing out
to INsight?

May we image imagine INlight?

In social intercourse we talk back
You say and I reply
This goes on for a lifetime
Tangling in double-talk and
in superficial responses
we practice oppositions

Our words are sounds before meanings
The Sanskrit *mantra* derives from *manana*
literally mind-ing or sound-ing
-ing brings a noun alive
Language nouns us

Weed   reed   plant
sentiment before sensing
beam tubes lightward   receiving

Hate fear confusion cannot stand
before INlighting
Thank the undying LIGHT

HOLD ARM OUT
AND POINT TO SOMETHING
THEN CURVE FINGERS
IN TO PALM

How do you do this?

Considering honestly
we must answer
"I don't know"

In this "don't know"
instantly experience
your potential true
whereof all this springs

By all means let us be
this honest with ourself

Play it seriously
as a child plays
experimentally

Some of us
some of the time
drown in current ways
of the world
tangle in mythopoetic
rigidities
and in old habits
too rarely coming to
the surface of bliss

In our new orienting
all cultures are ours
yet we need not submerge
us

"Would you say that
more simply?"

To take a step we WILL it
Without WILL we are loaded
with the wills of others
so we become slaves to
circumstance

"How do I free me?"

Innately we are already
wholly free

because of
400,000,000 years
you appear

16 NOW

Where is Buddha?
Where is Jesus?
Where are you?

Each forest tree
rests in
UNCHANGE

timeless spaceless IS

(The dream procession
of change would pull
us out of ME)

The easiest thing to do
seems to us the hardest
to let all self-imposed
pressures off our
nerve blood networks

To sit and look
to sit and listen
then to move
interests us

Even more interesting
may be to sit in
one's given breathflow
and let go with it
friend of birds and clouds

17 WHOLLY

MAP OF ME

unborn	subject	
	in ⟶	colors
preconceiving	here ⟶	shapes
	making ⟶	forms
in-finiting	up ⟶	things
	objects ⟵	ideas
reality	out there	

Eagle sees better
deer hears better
bear smells better
cat moves better
than we do
but we drive a car
and talk better
and better

We look into
countless objects
trying to find
the object
and pull apart
objects
trying to find
the subject

My instrument needs
some oil of lovingkindness
if I cannot sit at once
into utmost bliss

wholly
you

head and heart   not apart

IN a shower
wholly

stuck with a pin
wholly

Gesture
with both hands

Open
both arms in love

See
through both eyes

Hear
through both ears

Sit
on both sit bones

Play
games with both sides

Open
both sides of stem

Playing one-sidedly
one side of back   lower back
pains set in   soon gone with
equal use of both sides

walk
on

both
Feet

This playbook may be lived
in one breathflow

"How?"

Do you read and write?
Do you separate
mental from physical?

Mental and physical
are just words
for our silent reality
some name god allah
brahman   akua   the
great spirit   light
be-ing

Without birth no death
without death no birth
with birth death
something under over
through it

"What could it be?"

Your very life
the very life of be-ing
the only be-ing

Toss

6 sticks in air

Read

patterning there

You toss

you interpret

one image

worth 1,000 words

one presence

worth 1,000 pictures

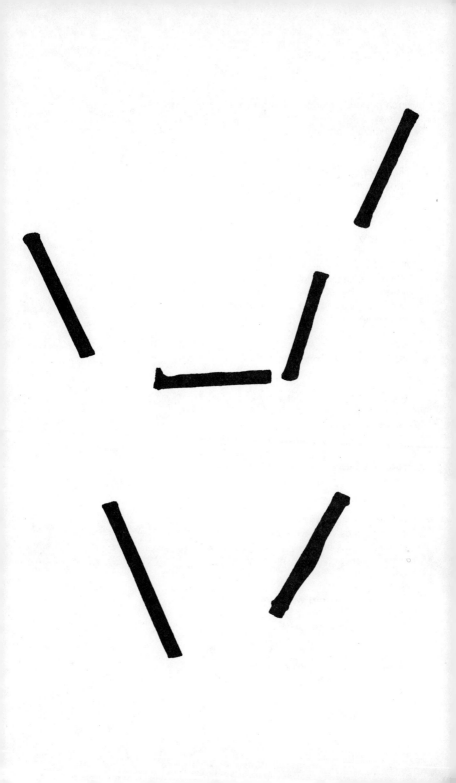

CALLIGRAPHY CLASS

1
Each gesture   motion   brushstroke
springs
originatively through you

2
Place paper   black ink   inkbrush
about as thick as a little finger
ink   and   water containers on a table

3
Sit wordless before them

4
When intellingly ready
lift brush   dip in water or in ink
and draw   (not push) across paper
soft paper

5
Place brush back on table

6
Contemplate   brushline
never done over
unique in uniquity

7
Each line best   raw   unexpecting
surprising

8
As weed writing on sky
as water   as wind write
as bird across air
witness you   there

9
Wash brush in cold water
Place on   shrine
for a next convocation

10
Give your priceless ink revelation
to a friend or stranger

Diploma

THIS CERTIFIES YOU AS A GRADUATE
OF THE SCHOOL OF LIGHT ALREADY
IN YOUR HEART ENTITLING YOU TO
TEACH FREE FLOW CALLIGRAPHY
IN THIS WORLD AND THE NEXT

_____   _reps_____

sign here

Shogi, the most interesting game in the world

Millions play shogi (*show-gee*, with hard *g*) in Japan, where games are printed in every afternoon newspaper. Here is a shogi board with pieces ready to play a game. The lines over each piece indicate which directions it can move. With these and the following rules anyone can learn the moves in a few minutes and enjoy the game for years.

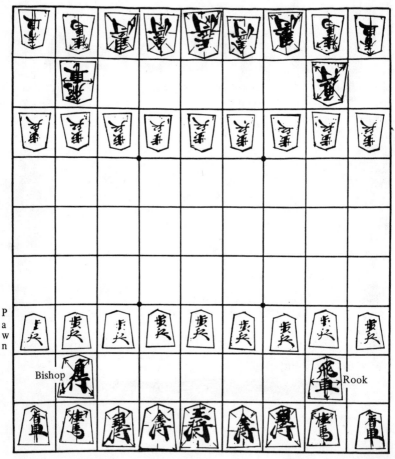

SPEAR KNIGHT SILVER GOLD KING GOLD SILVER KNIGHT SPEAR

Each piece points toward the opponent. Moves alternate. Toss for first move. Then winner of last game moves first. When a king is attacked, he is in "check" and you must immediately move him out of check or interpose another piece to protect him—either by moving one of your own already on the board or by "dropping" an already captured piece. If you cannot do so, it is "checkmate" and you have lost the game. You must not move the king so as to put him in check.

Move onto or over empty spaces. When an opposing piece stands in a space to which you can move, you may capture it and occupy its space. If you touch one of your own pieces, you must move it if possible or forfeit the game. If you touch one of your opponent's pieces, you must capture it if possible.

The four dots on the board mark your territory—your first three rows—and your opponent's first three rows. When any piece but the king or a gold moves into the far territory, it either is turned over and promoted to gold or it remains in its own power until it becomes gold on any later chosen move. A pawn always becomes gold on entering this area.

When the rook or bishop enters the opponent's area, it has the added power *on its next move* of capturing on or occupying any adjacent space—eight in all.

In shogi—unlike in chess, which it resembles—the pieces never die. When captured, they are yours to play for your side. When a piece is captured, turn it over and indicate its value (i.e., which directions it can move) on the back. Place the captured piece to the right of the board pointing toward your opponent so he can see what you might drop on him when it is your turn to move or drop. "Dropping" a captured piece—putting it back into play on your turn—constitutes a move in itself. The piece may be dropped on any chosen empty square on any chosen move, of course pointed toward your opponent.

If a piece is in enemy territory (the last three rows), you may not turn it over to promote it to gold until the following move, and even then you may choose not to turn it over at that time. (Gold, of course, does not turn over, as it is already gold.) Although pawn may move to put a king into checkmate, it may not be dropped on the board to do so.

You might like to draw a larger board than the one pictured here to play on—12⅜ inches high by 11 inches wide, with the 81 spaces, each 1⅜ inches high by 1½ inches wide—and mount it all on wood or cardboard.

Good shogi players defend first, then look for opportunities to attack. Often the king is moved to one side, protected by strong pieces, and the advance is begun from the other. Each player tries to penetrate the other's defenses. It need not take long to play a game, and each game is different.

While playing shogi, everything else is forgotten, so it is extremely refreshing. As in life, the pieces are moved about as the mover wills, but they get so excited moving from here to there, they forget the mover.

King (1)
Moves one space only in any direction—eight in all. Captures on this space, but cannot capture an opposing piece when it is guarded by another.

Gold (2)
Moves one space only in a direction pointed to by lines—six in all.

Silver (2)
Moves one space only in a direction pointed to by lines—five in all.

Knight (2)
Jumps two spaces ahead and one space to the right or left of its own. Does not jump sideways or backwards but may jump over any piece.

Spear (2)
Moves straight ahead any distance over empty spaces but never back.

Bishop (1)
Moves any distance over unoccupied spaces, diagonally only, forward or back.

Rook (1)
As strong a piece as the bishop. Moves any distance over empty spaces vertically or horizontally but not diagonally.

Pawn (9)
Moves one space straight ahead only and captures only straight ahead. Each player can have only one pawn at a time on any vertical line.

In playing a game   any game
we relate complex factors
watch all areas
include each possibility
in   overall view

This life-game also requires
such inclusion

No wonder our cells move
in   harmony with other cells
"Let me help" each cell affirms
"Me too"

As near as we know
each one insays ME
and self erases

Even in death ME dies
to become another ME

May ME includingly be the secret
of suns of suns powers
and so of ours?

The surgeon slices away a bit
of heart to find it continues beating
Cut into yet finer segments the beating
the rhythm   cellebrating continues

You are not your picture
not your name
nor your form
"Then what who am I?"

Honestly
silently
something declares
I
am

I WILL

become a
sunflower
seed

seed

into

tree

delight

tree

into

seed

light

You are the tree
Leaf "who me?"

You touch a book with 100% confidence
Reading a page you shift from touch to think
and have less than 100% confidence in it

"How do I restore this 100%?"
You've forgotten how

The newborn child responds
to skin-touch and falling
before seeing hearing

Pull right ear lobe
down with right hand

Now imagine pulling
left lobe down
with left hand

Note the effects as
similar

"Then why not imagine
everything we do?"

We do

Medicate?
Meditate

Meditate?
Celebrate

Picture writing as old as the hills
as clear as light

fence
good luck

rain

day   night

running water

paths crossing

teepee

bear tracks

sun
happiness

alert

bird

lightning

ceremonial
dance

mountain

valley

( ) juicing

present moon

moon

big

man

sun

later style sun

brightness

surprise
in your eyes

heart's breath

18 SHARING

We have a human obligation
to be primal   and   social
to feel   and   think
to abide   and   go do

Primally we are alive with the one life
socially we relate and transmit it to others

Low powered minimal effort:
SOFT NODDING   loosens back
OPENING HANDS   opens heart
LOWERING EYES   rests social mind
SOFT KNEED   gentles
MOVING   smoothing

You must act
Your breathflow
compels it

You speak on
outbreathflow
exert on
outbreathflow

You must receive
Your inbreathflow
in-vites it

Giving and receiving
the day night of life
one without the other
misses the point

THE BENEFICENCE

Do you have feet and toes?
Do you have hands and fingers?
Do you have eyes?
Are you in a position?
Do you move?
Can you tell what a bird flying
does for us?
Can you sense what the aroma
of a flower does for us?

If you answer is YES
to one of these questions
you are in
THE BENEFICENCE

May you abide in
the great peace

may your heart overflow
with love for our fount
of life

may your day be bright

"How?"
Step from the room of energy-charging rejuvenation
DEEP SLEEP
into the room of DREAM
wherein whatever we experience seems real and urgent
and then –
Step into this room of
WAKING DREAM
Here too whatever we experience seems real and urgent
while we are in it

Come into our wide room of DEEP WAKING
lasting reality wholly free of suffering   our room of
the self-luminous LIGHT   births and deaths and all
else included   in   unchanging bliss
HERE WE ARE

erase
Face

amazing
grace

Dear reader –

This book is put down
with life's blood
just for you

Probably you were as
puzzled as I was
and asked after
birth
"Why am I born?
What shall be
done about
this?"

My good parents seemed foreign to me
                    Gradually after 5 I became
                    socialized yet even then
                    self inquiry continued

                    I made Indian   Japanese   Chinese
                    friends and observed their variant
                    social systems
                    I met Buddha   Shankara and compared
                    them with the church Jesus
                    I refused to fight wars
                    but warring only got worse

Then I found I could not mind others' business
and when I did they only resented it
The best I could do was to use words as signs
pointing a way to town   To town?   Prefer
                    the forest

This brings
us
in a one-world
relationship
together

       You may ask:

"How do I make this
book work for me best?"

May I answer:
  Live it

Make some of its
directives yours
in your own best
      way

        Each one is
           best
         This means
            us

A radiant spaceman and beautiful
spacewoman appear on earth
"What do you do here?" they ask

The human receiving them shows a
life-size image on a screen and
explains

                    "We sleep"

"Yes" the spaceman replies "but we
have little need of that since we
have learned not to waste energy"

They are shown a moving picture
of two humans in violent sex
activity

                    "We procreate"

"But" comments the spacewoman
"are those panting turmoils
necessary to consciously create   *Cop, 1*
genius offspring"

They then see a black-robed group
of humans sitting on cushions

                    "We meditate"

"What goes on in them?" the spacewoman
asks

The human gives them a copy of
JUICING

Paul Reps is an American who has spent much of his adult life abroad, mainly in India, Norway, Japan. For years a student and teacher of comparative viewpoints, he is the author of many books of prose and poems, including *Ten Ways to Meditate; Sit In; Be: New Uses for the Human Instrument; As a Potato;* and *Square Sun Square Moon.* He also is the compiler of *Zen Flesh, Zen Bones: A Collection of Zen and Pre-Zen Writings.*